ABC

Animal Rhymes for You and Me

Giles Andreae

Illustrated by

David Wojtowycz

ORCHARD BOOKS

Aa Angelfish

Hello, I'm the angelfish, darling,

The prettiest thing in the sea.

What a shame there are no other creatures

As gorgeous and lovely as me!

ABC

Animal Rhymes for You and Me

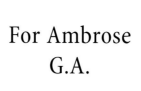

For Ambrose
G.A.

To Stacey, Will, Dixie and Dot
D.W.

ORCHARD BOOKS
338 Euston Road, London NW1 3BH
Orchard Books Australia
Level 17/207 Kent Street, Sydney, NSW 2000

First published in 2009 as *ABC Animal Jamboree* by Orchard Books
First published in paperback in 2010

Text © Purple Enterprises Ltd., a Coolabi company 1996, 1998, 2009
Illustrations © David Wojtowycz 1996, 1998, 2009

Includes material first published in *Rumble in the Jungle* (1996) and *Commotion in the Ocean* (1998)

The rights of Giles Andreae to be identified as the author and of David Wojtowycz to be identified
as the illustrator of this work have been asserted by them in accordance with the
Copyright, Designs and Patents Act, 1988.

A CIP catalogue record for this book is available from the British Library.

ISBN 978 1 40830 680 2

1 3 5 7 9 10 8 6 4 2
Printed in China

Orchard Books is a division of Hachette Children's Books,
an Hachette UK company.
www.hachette.co.uk

Bb

Boa Constrictor

The boa constrictor's a slippery snake
Who slithers and slides round his tree,
And when tasty animals wander too close
He squashes them slowly for tea.

Cc Crocodile

When animals come to the river to drink

I watch for a minute or two.

It's such a delight

To behold such a sight

That I can't resist chomping a few.

Dolphin

Dd

The wonderful thing about dolphins

Is hearing them trying to speak,

But it's not "How d'you do?"

Like I'd say to you

It's more of a "Click-whistle-squeak!"

Ee

Elephant

It's great to be an elephant,
All big and fat and round,
And wander through the jungle
Just elephing around.

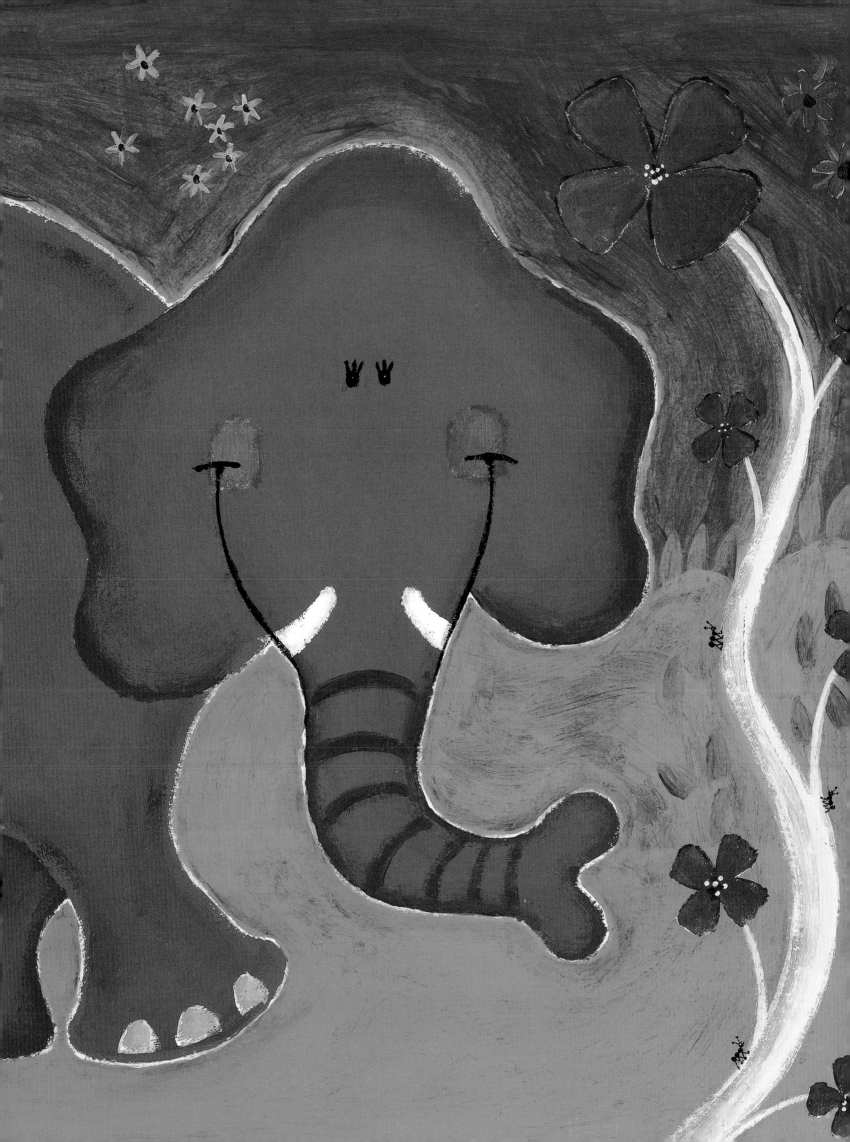

Ff

Frog

We may be green and slimy,
But I'm sure that you'll agree,
We're really great at hopping.
Can you hop as high as me?

Gg

Giraffe

Some animals laugh
At the gangly giraffe
But I hold my head up and feel proud.
I really don't care
When my head's in the air
And my cheek's getting kissed by a cloud.

Hh Hippopotamus

Hello, I'm a big, happy hippo.
I sleep in the sun to get hot,
And when I'm not sleeping
I mooch in the mud,
Which hippos like doing a lot.

Iguana

We are both green iguanas,

Our bodies are covered with scales.

We've also got really cool spines down our backs

Which run to the ends of our tails!

Ii

Jj

Jellyfish

The jellyfish just loves to jiggle,
Which other fish think is quite dumb.
She knows that it's not all that useful,
But jiggling's very good fun.

Kangaroo

Kk

I'm the bouncy kangaroo.

Pleased to meet you! How d'you do?

And who's inside my pouch? That's right . . .

It's Baby Joey holding tight!

Ll

rrrr

Lion

The lion's the king of the jungle,
Just listen how loudly he roars!
Every animal quivers
And shudders and shivers
As soon as he opens his jaws.

Mm Monkey

It's great to be a monkey,
Swinging through the trees,
And if we can't find nuts to eat
We munch each other's fleas!

Narwhal

Nn

The narwhal has a horn-like tusk
And so he seems to be
The ocean's swimming unicorn,
A marvel of the sea!

Oo Octopus

Having eight arms can be useful,

You may think it looks a bit funny,

But it helps me to hold all my children

And tickle each one on the tummy.

P p

Penguin

We waddle about on our icebergs,
Which makes our feet slither and slide,
And when we get close to the water
We leap with a splosh off the side.

Qq

Quetzal

My tail feathers shimmer in glorious green
And look at my splendid red chest.
Of all the most beautiful birds that you've seen
You must admit I am the best!

Rhinoceros

Rr

The ravenous rhino

Is big, strong and tough,

But his skin is all baggy and flappy,

Which means that there's plenty

Of room for his lunch,

And that makes him terribly happy.

Ss Shark

I swim with a grin up to greet you,
See how my jaws open wide.
Why don't you come a bit closer?
Please, take a good look inside . . .

Tiger

Tt

Beware of the terrible tiger,
You don't always know when he's near,
But his eyes shine like lights
Through the blackest of nights,
And his growl makes you tremble with fear.

Uu

Umbrella Bird

My head has a crest of black feathers,
So when I look up at the sky
And see that it's raining
Instead of complaining
I just spread them out and keep dry!

Vulture

Vv

See me soaring gracefully
Across the clear blue sky,
Looking out for tasty treats
That catch my beady eye!

Ww

There's no other beast on the planet
As big as the giant blue whale.

He measures a massive one hundred feet long
From his head to the tip of his tail.

Xx

X-ray Fish

We like to swim around in shoals
And any food will do us.
Oh yes, we're called the X-ray fish
As you can see right through us!

Yak

We live up in the mountains
Where the land is cold and bare,
So to keep us warm and cosy
We grow thick, long, shaggy hair!

Zz

Zebra

I could have been grey like a donkey

Or brown like my cousin the mule,

But instead I've got stripes

Which my ladyfriend likes

As they make me look handsome and cool.